WYMOND[...]

a century remembered

PHILIP YAXLEY

NOSTALGIA *Publications*

TOFTWOOD • DEREHAM • NORFOLK

Published by:
NOSTALGIA PUBLICATIONS
(Terry Davy)
7 Elm Park, Toftwood,
Dereham, Norfolk
NR19 1NB

First impression: June 1999

© Philip Yaxley

ISBN 0 947630 26 0

Design and typesetting:
NOSTALGIA PUBLICATIONS

Printed by:
BARNWELL'S OF AYLSHAM
Penfold Street,
Aylsham, Norfolk,
NR11 6ET

ILLUSTRATIONS

Front Cover - *(Top)* The Market Place presents a placid scene as a cyclist passes by in August 1932. Next to the coach on the right is "Chippy" Harwood's fish and chip van.

(Bottom) Robert Shorten & Son were no doubt proud of their new Model T Ford delivery van in the 1920s.

Title Page - *(Top)* Gypsies passing quietly through the town in the 1930s. In 1615, gypsies had been hung in Norwich for allegedly starting Wymondham's Great Fire that year.

(Centre) Hampers of rough plucked turkeys on a dray, pulled by a traction engine, starting out in 1913 from Stanfield Hall Farm to London for the Christmas market.

(Bottom) Taken in the grounds of Wattlefield Hall in the 1920s, Mrs. M. Routh Clarke stands beside her new Austin Chummy Tourer, while Herbert Smith leads a horse and cart.

Contents

A contrast in transport in March 1996. Britannia 70000, the engine which hauled the Broadsman for many years, pulls a specially commissioned train from Finsbury Park, London, to Norwich, whilst in the background traffic hurries along the stretch of the dualled A11 between Wymondham and Cringleford, which had been opened in 1987. The train stopped at Wymondham as part of the station's 150th anniversary celebrations.

Introduction

"We are moving ahead towards that millennium still far away on the horizon. Progress is slow, but we believe sure, and ere long we shall one and all rejoice in a free and happy Wymondham".

These words were written by a newspaper commentator in 1913! The writer had expectations of improvements in the town, perhaps in the running of its affairs and in the everyday lives of its folk. With dramatic technological and social advances, there has certainly been more change in the last hundred years than in all the previous two thousand. Generally, today, people are healthier, live longer and are better off.

In Wymondham the century has seen old industries like brushmaking disappear and many people turning to small concerns, Lotus Cars and Norwich for employment. Once important buildings like the King's Head Inn have been demolished, while vast housing estates have sprung up to accommodate an ever increasing population.

Certainly, there has been much progress in many fields through the 20th century, but whether the hopes of that 1913 scribe have been realised is a matter for conjecture.

Acknowledgements

I wish to record my special thanks to the staff of the Eastern Counties Newspapers Library, the Norfolk Studies Library and Janet Smith, the Wymondham Archivist, all of whom have been most helpful.

Among many others who have either lent photographs or offered snippets of information I should specially like to mention Alastair Florance, Mary Ayton, Bob Bagshaw, Richard Barham, Mary Barnicoat, Tony Bradstreet, Joan Bunn, Pat Buttolph, Jean Clarke, Jill Clarke, Gerry Collins, Alan Coombe, Ann Edwards, Margaret Edwards, Ted Fowler, Doug Fulcher, Rev. Canon Brian Gant, Alan Garwood, George Gosling, John Hannant, Mrs C. Harmer, Janet Harwood, Ann Hoare, Diana Hockaday, Peter Henderson, Charles Leather, George Mabbutt, Don McLauchlan, Colin Morley, Tim Semmence, Peggy Sheldrake, David Smith, John Speakman, Mary Standley, John Staveley, Peter Wharton, Dennis Whitehead, John Wood, Joy Young.

Special acknowledgement must be given to the following whose photographs I have reproduced with their kind permission:

Richard Bartram - 72T, 76T, 79T, 79B, 80B, 81T, 82T, 82B, 83B, 84T, 84B, 87B, 90T, 90B

Terry Burchell - 3, 92B, 93T, 93B

Philip Chapman - 56, 58T, 58B, 62, 64B, 65T

Eastern Counties Newspapers - 40T, 51T, 52T, 54B, 61T, 61B, 65B, 66B, 69T, 69B, 73B, 74B, 80T, 81B, 83T, 85T, 89B

Ruth Dwornik - 72B

Group Lotus Limited - 76B

Colin Morley - 92T

Norfolk Library & Information Service - 34T

George Plunkett - 60B

South Norfolk Council - 88T

Wymondham Heritage Museum - 6T, 91B

Wymondham Photographic - 89T, 91B

Wymondham Town Archive - 25T, 55T, 64T, 66T, 67B, 70

I have endeavoured to trace all copyright holders and if I have not contacted anyone please accept my apologies.

I would like to thank Richard Barham for reading the text, Terry Burchell for photographic work and my wife Wendy and daughter Joanne for word-processor duties and bearing with me whilst this work was researched and compiled.

Chapter One

The Edwardian Era

THE EDWARDIAN ERA saw the British Empire at its zenith. It was a time of much patriotic fervour and the picture shows the town decorated in 1909 for the annual show organised by the Wymondham Agricultural Society, which had been founded four years earlier. These shows were held up to the Great War on a ground off Norwich Road, where the High School now stands.

Apart from many agricultural related occupations, like blacksmith, work within the town was mainly provided by brushmaking, sawmills, stone-pits, a weaving factory, domestic service and, up to 1908, the boot and shoe concern of P. Haldinstein & Son in Market Street.

Wymondham's affairs were almost exclusively run by males from the parish's elite, but there was still hardship amongst the lower classes. However, radical changes were afoot and the Edwardian period was the last of the old order.

An election card issued by Sir Frederick Wilson (Liberal) in the "Khaki" election of 1900. Wilson had held the Mid-Norfolk constituency, in which Wymondham was then placed, since 1895 and he retained it against William Boyle (Conservative). Lord Wodehouse won the seat again for the Liberals in 1906, before Boyle captured it in 1910 from W. R. Lester, a new Liberal candidate.

VOTE FOR WILSON,
A NORFOLK MAN FOR NORFOLK.

Printed and Published by H. G. Stone, Wymondham.

The brass band of the F(Wymondham) Company of the 4th Volunteer Battalion of the Norfolk Regiment at the turn of the century. Behind the drum is Charles Robert Ayton and the man in civilian clothes is Algernon S. Wilde, the bandmaster. Ayton held many public offices, as well as serving as Parish Clerk. Several Wymondham Volunteers served in the Boer War and the Peace of 1902 was greeted with great rejoicing in the town.

6

A tranquil traffic-free Market Street circa 1912. To commemorate Edward VII's coronation in 1902, the Parish Council arranged for 2,500 yards of kerbing to be laid along the town's streets. Street lighting was provided by the Wymondham Gas and Coke Co Ltd, whose works were near the Fairland. In the photograph, Walter Mace was a boot maker and Samuel Pluck a men's outfitter.

No planning restrictions on signage! Josiah Wade, a plumber and painter of Damgate, was proud of the new sign placed on his house in the Spring of 1908. In 1912, a new direction post was erected on the Market Place, but many people felt it was unsightly and should be removed. Nothing was done and some wags took the law into their own hands and obliterated the lettering with tar.

The Wymondham Troop of Boy Scouts parading on the Market Place in September 1910. The Scouts' organisation had been founded by General Sir Robert Baden-Powell in 1908 and, soon after, the Wymondham Troop was formed. On the left is the scoutmaster, Sergeant-Major J. M. Webster, and on the right Frank Alpe, an assistant scoutmaster. Alpe practised as a barrister on the South-Eastern circuit and at the Old Bailey before being made Judge of the Norwich Guildhall Court in 1939. In 1951 he was appointed Recorder of Yarmouth.

The Post Office staff at their Market Street premises soon after Claude Firman, the lad on the left with a bicycle, joined them as a messenger boy in June 1903. Until they were 18 years old, messenger boys earned five shillings a week. When Firman joined he could not ride a bike and had to walk twenty miles on the starting day, but he spent his first wages buying an "old boneshaker", on which he quickly mastered the art.

Workers in a stone-pit at Silfield in 1914. Over 200 men were employed in such pits around Wymondham and up to 40 truck loads of flints were leaving the town's railway station each day for destinations all over Eastern England. The pits were mostly run by Charles Ayton, who had realised the adhesive properties of Wymondham's "cannon-shot" gravel for road-building purposes. The Ayton Asphalt Company still survives today.

Children posing in Damgate without fear of traffic. On the left, a gentleman stands in the doorway of the Two Brewers, which also incorporated a greengrocer's shop. It was one of several public houses in the street at a time when the numerous pubs and beerhouses of the town provided most of the populace with their social life. On the right, where the ladder stands, was Herbert Cawdron's off-licence.

9

Cycling was popular, both as a form of transport and as a sport. Before taking over this shop on the corner of Queen's Street around 1910, Bert Middleton had worked from premises on the Market Place, which were later incorporated into the Co-op, and in Fairland Street. In 1906 the prices of cycles were being quoted as between £5 10s (£5.50) and £12, a big slice of a farm worker's wages.

John Slaughter stands in front of one of the town's first cars, possibly a Wolseley or a Wolseley-Siddeley. The motor dates from about 1907-10, but the picture was taken later in the yard of the King's Head Inn, where the car had been used for a taxi service to the railway station. Around 1906, Maurice Hughes and George Lowe, local doctors, became the first Wymondham people to own cars, John Clarke chauffeuring for the latter. In 1912, a car belonging to Captain Cautley at Abbotsford went up in flames when a lad, who was cleaning it, took a lamp too close to the petrol tank!

Pictured in 1912, the Wymondham Union Co-operative Society bakery claimed it provided "the loaf creamy crumb". The Co-op shop on the Market Place was noted for its "divi" and boasted a drapery and grocery, then later also a butchery and tailoring department. In the early 1900s, some dedicated Tories would not patronise the Co-op as "it was not of their persuasion".

Like the Co-op, the International Tea Company's Stores (later the International), situated on the side of the Market Place, used a horse-drawn cart to make deliveries around the town and its environs. Several local dairies delivered milk, which was served from a churn, while there were numerous licensed hawkers plying their wares.

The fifteenth annual show of the Wymondham and District Ornithological Society was held at the Town Hall in Town Green over two days in November 1907. The exhibits, which included poultry, pigeons, rabbits, canaries and other cage birds, were described as "of a very high order indeed". The Town Hall, which now houses an antiques centre and the snooker club, was used for concerts, dances and election meetings.

Boys from the Watts' Naval Training School performing a drill at the town's Whit Thursday Sports on the King's Head Meadow in 1908. With packed trains arriving at Wymondham station, spectators flocked to the sports from around the County and further afield. Cycle races were popular and that year the one mile bicycle handicap featured an "exciting incident", when one competitor was hurled with his bicycle amongst spectators at the Norwich end of the ground.

When the sports were dropped in 1909, "Old Chowes" Blazey, a well-known character, paraded the town wearing a silk top hat and frock coat with a board proclaiming "Wymondham is Dead, Sports Suicide". He is seen here on Damgate Bridge with another board after a walk to Attleborough, where sports were still held.

Posing with the prizes, the sports committee pictured around 1912 when the annual sports were revived. In the front row with his bell is Jesse Harvey, the town crier. He announced the sports results, public notices and all manner of events. After his death in 1914, he was succeeded in the bellman's role by his son, also Jesse, who held the office until the Second World War.

13

There was great excitement when King Edward VII passed through Wymondham on the morning of 25 October 1909. The schoolchildren from Browick Road and Silfield Public Elementary Schools were marched down to the Market Place and joined the Church Choir in singing the first verse of the national anthem as the monarch's car approached. Their singing was drowned by the loud cheering, but the King "graciously acknowledged the expressions of loyalty".

A united service on the Market Place was one of many events held on 22 June 1911 to celebrate the coronation of King George V. There were rural sports on the King's Head Meadow and a tea at Abbotsford for the schoolchildren, who were each presented with a coronation mug. After a decorated cycle parade, the day concluded with dancing and fireworks on the King's Head Meadow.

The aftermath of a serious fire at the wood-turning factory of Robert Semmence & Son at Cavick in October 1907. The turning shops, engine and boiler house were gutted; and but for the admirable work of the Wymondham Fire Brigade, founded in 1882, much more damage would have resulted. The proximity of the River Tiffey proved crucial. Other big fires, like that which destroyed Parker's Stores in Market Street in 1901, kept Wymondham's firemen busy.

The great flood of Monday 26 August 1912 caused widespread damage and great distress in Wymondham. Much of the town was under water as the River Tiffey burst its banks and "the houses of Hubbard and Nicholls" in Damgate, shown here, were devastated by the swirling waters. A flood relief fund was set up to provide some compensation for the many victims.

Cabs waiting for passengers at the railway station. Wymondham was a busy junction on the Norwich to Cambridge and Ely line, with one branch line to Dereham, Fakenham and Wells and another to Ashwellthorpe and Forncett. Both the King's Head and the Temperance Hotel, run by Charles Mallows then later his daughters Minnie and Kitty in Middleton Street, ran cabs to meet every train. The fare to town was one shilling (5p).

The Abbey Church while undergoing a major restoration between 1901 and 1905. A gigantic crack, which could accommodate a man, had appeared in the West tower. Various events were staged to raise funds for the work, including a Grand Bazaar at Abbotsford (1905), featuring the band of the Royal Scots Greys, and Industrial Exhibitions, which were held in the Vicarage Room. Mrs Clara Willett, daughter of a former Vicar, contributed the immense sum of £14,000.

The foundation stone for the Baptist Church in Queen's Street was laid by Sir George White, M.P. for North-West Norfolk, during this ceremony in May 1909. The Church was built by Benjamin Blazey's local firm and the bricklayers, who included William Baker and Bob Alderton, earned 9d(4p) an hour for a 59 hour week. In the right background can be seen R. B. Hovell and Company's horsehair weaving factory.

In 1913 the Rev. Edwin Russell (pictured), a respected Congregational Church minister, opposed William Fryer in a heated County Council election, which highlighted the political rivalry between the established Church and the Nonconformists. The campaign arguments are too complex to discuss here, but on the morning of the poll Wymondham folk woke to find the pavements in Market Street tarred with the words "Russell Liar". Mr Fryer was not responsible for this outrage and won the election 643-501.

Chapter Two

The Great War

IN EARLY AUGUST 1914, men were called off tennis courts, which were situated on the old Grammar School's playing-field, now occupied by the High School on Norwich Road. World War One had been declared and they hurried to Norwich to register for army service. Some 750 Wymondham men enlisted voluntarily in the early days of the war and another 450 joined up in 1916.

Soon after the declaration, the Wymondham Miniature Rifle Club called a public meeting in the King's Head Inn to offer the menfolk "with a patriotic spirit the chance to learn to shoot". Indeed, the townsfolk would contribute to the war effort in several ways.

In November 1914 the 4th Service Battalion of the Essex Regiment arrived in Wymondham and the picture shows a group of the regiment's "gunners" with their mascot goat in Vicar Street.

A military funeral, almost certainly of one of the Essex Regiment, leaves Kimberley Street for the cemetery. Many of the Essex contingent were billeted in the Norwich Road area and enjoyed fine hospitality from the townsfolk. No doubt they were sorry to leave the town at the end of January 1915.

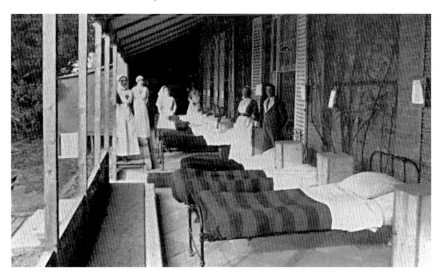

In November 1914, a Red Cross (Voluntary Aid Detachment) Hospital was opened in the Vicarage Room in Church Street, then in May 1915, in order to meet a demand for more beds, Captain and Mrs Cautley offered part of their Vicar Street home at Abbotsford. There, the large veranda, pictured here, was added for "open-air patients". The hospital's commandant was Mrs Rose Martin-Jones, the Vicar's wife, and during the war over 800 patients were treated.

A stack of either beans or lucerne being built at Stalworthy's Farm, Suton, around the end of the war. Despite the war life went on and in the middle of the group is a soldier, perhaps earning some extra pocket money. During the conflict much work at home was left to women and older men. Although a Zeppelin dropped a bomb at Silfield, no damage was done and Wymondham remained unscathed.

Men, probably painters, posing up a chimney at the Lady's Lane factory of S. D. Page & Sons (later to become the Briton Brush Company) in 1915. The chimney was used to release fumes from the gas plant. During the war S. D. Page & Sons made four million brushes for the army and navy, in spite of losing many men to the services. Pages had moved to Wymondham from Norwich in 1886.

YOUR KING AND COUNTRY THANK YOU
Friends at Wicklewood will remember every Sailor and Soldier this Christmastide.

Coy. Sergt Maj: H. Daniels V.C.
2nd Batt: Rifle Brigade.

A patriotic card issued by Wicklewood Ladies' War Committee, which was organised in the village by the Rev. Mansbridge, the Vicar. No doubt such cards, together with items like Balaclavas and socks, knitted by the ladies, were sent in parcels of comforts to local menfolk serving their King and Country.

Company Sergeant-Major Harry Daniels was born in Wymondham in 1884, the son of a Market Street baker, though he later lived in Norwich. He won the V.C. for "conspicuous bravery" on 12 March 1915 at Neuve Chapelle and, during his triumphal return to Norwich three months later, he visited his brother-in-law, Mr E. A. Blyth of Elm Terrace, and the V.A.D. hospital in the town.

Wymondham's Lieutenant Malcolm Ayton, received the M.C. for gallantry at Vimy Ridge. Hence the name of a road off Norwich Road in the town.

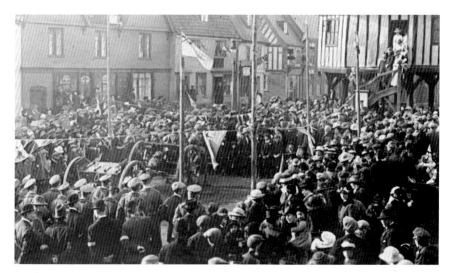

Crowds gather round an eighteen pounder field gun, which had seen service in France, during a "Feed the Guns" week to raise money for the war effort in November 1918. It was ironic that the week of events, which included a baseball match between American teams on the King's Head Meadow, was held at the time the Armistice was signed.

A united service on the Fairland was part of the Peace Celebrations on Saturday 19 July 1919. On that gloriously fine day, events included a dinner for the discharged men, a tea for the children, a fancy dress cycle parade and rural sports. But for some, the celebrations were tempered by sadness. One hundred and forty-two Wymondham menfolk had lost their lives and about 400 had been wounded.

Chapter Three
The Roaring Twenties

IN THE EXCITING TWENTIES people felt more liberated and the cinema, dancing and sport were all in vogue. Working folk were able to enjoy excursions in motor coaches and the Wymondham Town Band pose by the side of a United charabanc in Market Street. Veteran musician Arthur Farrow stands second from the left. In 1920 the United Automobile Services Limited were advertising trips from Norwich to Attleborough via Wymondham, "a quiet little town"; and the Service 12, which ran along that route, was established. The company was absorbed by Eastern Counties Omnibus Company Limited in 1931.

In 1922 the Co-operative Wholesale Society Limited set up a brush factory at the Poynt Sawmills off Chapel Lane, which it had acquired in 1917, while the Briton Brush Company closed its Norwich and Tottenham (London) works later in the decade to concentrate production at Wymondham. With some London workers moving to Norfolk, brushmaking became unquestionably the town's main employment.

Looking across from the Park Lane direction to Wymondham's first council houses soon after they had been built at Silfield Crescent between 1919 and 1921. Following Prime Minister David Lloyd George's slogan of "Homes fit for heroes" in the 1918 election campaign, the 1919 Housing Act had put the onus on district councils to provide houses for working people. Further council houses were erected elsewhere in the town like Browick Road and Vimy Ridge.

Major H. L. Cautley addressing a large gathering after the unveiling of Wymondham's War Memorial at Town Green in July 1921. A procession, which included the local Voluntary Aid Detachment of Red Cross Nurses, the Girl Guides, the Boy Scouts and ex-servicemen, marched from Abbotsford to the memorial for the unveiling and service of dedication. After the service, relations of the fallen men placed wreaths at the front of the monument.

24

William Blyth, pictured in the doorway of his family's baker's and grocer's shop in Friarscroft Lane about 1920. In the days before advertising in the mass media, the enamel signs on the side were essential; and Blyth's shop, like that of George Harwood's general stores further up Friarscroft Lane, was just one of numerous small retail outlets which thrived in the town's back streets.

The Damgate butcher's shop of J. R. Wharton & Son soon after the Great War and possibly in the run-up to Christmas. Whartons had established the shop in 1890, took on an additional one in Town Green in 1914, then moved the business to Market Street in 1938. In the photograph, Tom Wharton stands between Popsey Walker, the boy, and Reggie Wharton.

Wymondham Cricket Club who won the Saturday Norfolk Junior Cup in 1920 with a convincing 86 runs victory over Boulton & Paul in the final at Lakenham. In the middle of the back row is Philip Fryer, who played for Norfolk, while Doctor George Gaynor and Malcolm Ayton are first left and third from the left in the middle row. In the 1920-21 season Wymondham Town F.C. became champions of the strong Norwich & District Football League.

The all-local cast of the pantomime Jack of Hearts, which was presented at the Town Hall (i.e. Picture House) in early January 1924. Una Chatterton played Jack of Hearts and Tom Thackeray was the town crier. The success of this production led some months later to the formation of the Wymondham Amateur Theatrical Society, which staged further pantomimes and plays throughout the Twenties and into the early Thirties.

The Wymondham dancing club at its annual dance in the mid-1920s. It was the Jazz Age of the flapper and the Charleston was the rage. The club was organised by James Underwood (fifth from the left in the front row) and his wife Connie (seventh from the left in the second row). The classes were held in the Vicarage Room and music was invariably provided by the increasingly popular gramophone.

Anyone for tennis? With an urn on the table, players enjoy a typical tennis tea on courts off Norwich Road in the late 1920s. Fourth from the right wearing a cap is Cyril Ayton, who had the courts laid in an old gravel pit jointly owned with his brother Malcolm. A little later the site was developed to include a green for the Priory Park Bowling Club, which became the famous Wymondham Dell.

Wymondham, Dereham & District Laundry vans collected and delivered weekly in the locality. The business had been established in premises off Cock Street in the 1890s and had moved to Norwich Road in 1913. The photograph was taken outside Cavick House, some time just after the Great War.

A Model T. Ford motor coach belonging to H. Semmence & Co at Ringland Hills around 1927. It was just after the Great War that Herbert Semmence set up the company at Norwich Road, where a motor garage and workshops were built and from which a haulage business was run. In the Twenties, Semmences were advertising "saloon buses, charabancs, closed and open cars for hire any time during day or night".

Farm workers at Low Street, Wicklewood, during their "Great Strike" over wage reductions in the Spring of 1923. Vast crowds of strikers attended meetings in Kimberley Park, where they were addressed by the Earl of Kimberley, Labour's first peer. The action lasted a month and there were no winners, but it did strengthen the National Union of Agricultural Workers, whose President from 1928 (to 1961) was Wymondham's Edwin Gooch. There were a number of cases before the Wymondham Magistrates' Court arising out of the strike.

A train, pulled by a Claud Hamilton engine, draws into Wymondham Station in 1924. Newspapers were delivered from W. H. Smith & Son's bookstall, but deliveries, like those of coal, were restricted during the 1926 General Strike. The nine-day strike disorganised rail services and, except for the stationmaster, three porters and two clerks, the 30 odd staff at Wymondham Station all walked out. A prominent local farmer did duty as a signalman and a volunteer guard was spotted wearing a bowler hat!

The sawmills of the Briton Brush Company were completely gutted by a fire, which broke out on a September evening in 1924. In fighting the blaze, the Wymondham Brigade was assisted by two motor engines from Norwich. Even so, many thousands of pounds worth of damage was incurred and a considerable number of men were temporarily thrown out of work.

The funeral of Alderman William B. Fryer, who farmed at Browick Hall, in April 1926. With a farm wagon as the hearse, the cortège passes up Market Street on its way from the Abbey Church to the cemetery. Mr Fryer's long record of public service included the offices of county councillor, magistrate and churchwarden. In the picture, the Men's Club is on the immediate left with the Post Office next to it.

Mothers and their offspring, who attended Doctor Alex Agnew's monthly baby clinic, gather in the garden of Robert V. Reyner's Church Street home in 1928. Mr Reyner is on the left and Doctor Agnew on the right. Doctor Agnew lived in the Red House, now the Abbey Hotel, and he was particularly concerned with pre-school health. Mr Reyner, who was highly prominent in Church and Parish affairs, died in 1933.

Labour Party workers outside the Labour Institute after the announcement of the South Norfolk result in the 1929 General Election in which their candidate George Young (eighth from the left in the second row) had lost to James Christie (National Conservative) by a 2292 majority. On Mr Young's right are Ethel Gooch, Mrs Young and Edwin Gooch. The Labour Institute, which had been opened in Church Street by the Earl of Kimberley in 1919, now forms part of the Abbey Hotel complex.

Chapter Four
The Depressing Thirties

M IDDLETON STREET soon after the Urban District Council offices, seen on the left, were opened in a former Georgian house in 1938. The offices befitted a town, which in 1935 had been elevated to Urban District status with greater control over its own affairs. For much of the decade Edwin Gooch was the town council's chairman and his wife Ethel was the local county councillor. The contribution these two made to Wymondham's affairs was immense.

Among several important developments were the installation of a water and sewerage scheme (1933) and the opening of a Senior School, now part of the High School on Norwich Road, (1939). In 1937 public conveniences were built on the Market Place.

Nationally high unemployment was devastating and, with the advent of other materials for road-building, stone pit workers in Wymondham were among many out of work. However, with the brush works busy and projects like the water and sewerage scheme absorbing much labour, albeit temporarily, the town was perhaps more fortunate than others in Norfolk.

Market Street in June 1932 during the laying of the town's water and sewerage systems. For several weeks the town's main streets were closed, but the scheme did provide welcome work for some of the many unemployed men. By late May 1933, the systems were brought into use, though the official opening ceremonies at the High Oak waterworks and the Chapel Lane sewerage works did not take place until 13 June that year.

Members of the Parish Council's recreation ground committee watching progress during the week in October 1934 when construction of the recreation ground at Browick Road began. Disused gravel pits covering ten acres had been purchased for £100 and unemployed men were used in the work. Those watching are James Underwood, W. R. Purchase, A. W. Hobbs the surveyor, Henry Elkins, Edwin Gooch, Harry Clarke and G. Hector.

Schoolboys helping to unload books for the new County Library branch at the Market Cross in May 1930. Studying some of the volumes are the Town Library Committee, including Harry Clarke who is looking over Edwin Gooch's shoulder. The library was free to residents except for 2d (1p) registration fee. It started with 200 members, but by April 1931, when it moved to Becket's Chapel, it had 771. It changed to the chapel as a result of fears for the safety of the Market Cross.

Pupils at the Wymondham Boys' Central School at Browick Road celebrating the introduction of a milk scheme in February 1931. The children could purchase a third of a pint bottle of "Grade A" milk daily for a penny. Doctor Alex Agnew, the Medical Officer of Health for the Forehoe District, had promoted the scheme, which proved popular with boys and girls at the Central Schools as well as Norwich Common School.

Local lads at Wymondham's heated swimming bath at Brewery Lane soon after it was opened by owner William Smith in July 1931. It was sited in part of the old brewery premises and a huge beer vat was believed to have formed the pool! The opening was celebrated with a display by the Heigham Penguin Swimming Club from Norwich; and many people from the city and its surrounds availed themselves of the facility. It finally closed in 1953.

Members of the Wymondham and District Rifle Club in action in October 1934. For a long time the club's outdoor range was in gravel pits at Browick Road with its indoor headquarters in the Drill Hall at Pople Street. The marksmen are, left to right, J. Long, C. Fowler, A. Proctor and J. Kerridge. Watching them is Fred Roope, who completed 45 years as secretary of the club in 1960 at the age of 91!

People dispersing from a united church service, which was held on the Fairland to mark the Silver Jubilee of King George V on 6 May 1935. During an eventful day, children participated in maypole dancing and sports on the King's Head Meadow before enjoying tea in either the Fairland or Women's Institute Halls. In the evening, a parade round the town of fancy dress competitors, decorated cycles and vehicles provided much amusement.

The Briton Brush Company's annual Summer outing to Skegness around 1935. Occasions like this, together with the success of its men's football side and women's hockey team, reflected the excellent community spirit within the company in the inter-war years. The factory also boasted its own concert troupe and even a dance band called The Hurbs. The railwayman beside the train is Bob Allcock and the man with his hand raised is Edgar Bilner.

Vans from Chas. H. Standley & Son, at the "Little Dustpan" ironmongery in Town Green, assembled opposite the shop, ready to participate in the town's first ever carnival parade in 1936. The wireless was becoming increasingly popular and about 1930 Standleys had incorporated a radio department selling K.B. receivers, which the vans were advertising. One of the first attempts at television reception in the county occurred in a darkened room in Mr Walter Giles's house at Wymondham in November 1937. An attending newspaper reporter described the results as "remarkable".

The Women's Institute Hall was packed for a schoolgirls' tea to celebrate the coronation of King George VI and Queen Elizabeth on 12 May 1937. The boys were entertained at the Fairland Hall. Bad weather caused many of the planned festivities to be cancelled; and some events like the kiddies' sports were held a week later. Once inside the hall, the children soon forgot about the teeming rain outside as they tucked into sandwiches, cakes and pastries.

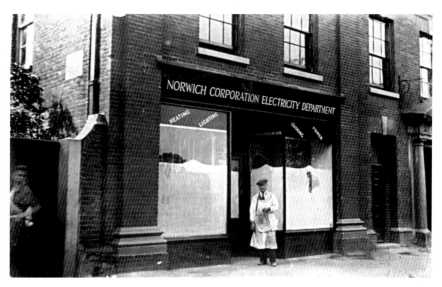

The Norwich Corporation Electricity Department's showroom soon after it had been opened in part of Caius House, an early Georgian dwelling, in 1933. The Reverend Frederic Jarvis, the Vicar, did not approve and commented in the parish magazine, "Caius House has been ruined by shop fronts". With nationalisation of electricity in 1948, the Eastern Electricity Board took over, but the Wymondham shop and its adjacent stores were closed in 1996.

Leslie Albert Fiske outside his Market Street barber's shop - always a good place to hear the latest local gossip. Fiske had established his men's hairdressing business in the front room of a house in Damgate, but moved it to Market Street at the end of the 1920s. He ran the business until retirement in 1953 and some of his experiences were later recalled in "Tales from a Barber's Shop", written by his son Cyril.

An impressive group of Wymondham police officers about 1934. In the middle of the front row is Superintendent Oscar Carter, while on the left with a motor cycle is P.C. Bob "Speed-cop" White, a familiar figure in the district. The photograph was taken in the yard of the Bridewell complex, which included the police station, the courtroom, the superintendent's house and other accommodation. All this changed in 1963 when a new police station was built near the Fairland.

The Dennis "Ace" fire engine on Mr Cautley's meadow, where there was a demonstration of its capabilities before the Urban District Council purchased it in November 1935. The motorised appliance, boasting a self-propelled pump with a capacity of 350-450 gallons per minute, replaced the old manual pumps. Including extras, like a hose and an escape ladder, it cost a total of £971:17s (£971.85) and served the Wymondham Fire Brigade until 1956.

The Regal Cinema on its opening day in March 1937. The first film shown was "Swing Time", starring the great Ginger Rogers and Fred Astaire, then this was followed by "Poor Little Rich Girl", featuring child star sensation Shirley Temple. Harold Crane was appointed the first resident manager of the Regal, which was on the Bostock Cinema Circuit, and he was followed about four years later by Bert Caley, who spent a lifetime in the service of cinemas.

The Wymondham Laundry on Norwich Road shortly after its new frontage and impressive 87-foot tall chimney had been built in 1938. At that time, it had a staff of well over 50 and serviced a wide area, which included Watton and Thetford. With their hampers of laundry, the gentry were good customers. The laundry closed in September 1969 and the work was transferred to the Swan Laundry in Norwich.

Chapter Five

The Second World War

WYMONDHAM PRESENTED A CALM APPEARANCE in that long hot Summer of 1939. However, for some time, the townsfolk had been making preparations for a war, which they hoped would never really happen.

An Air Raid Precautions Committee had been meeting regularly since May 1938 and, from time to time, blackout exercises and fire drills had been practised. In the September gas masks were available, while by January 1939 60 A.R.P. wardens had been enrolled, of whom 44 were fully trained.

Sandbag revetments were built at strategic points and big trenches dug for refuge should air attacks occur. Shelters too were ordered. In the Spring of 1939 arrangements for the billeting and welfare of the expected influx of evacuees began to be made. With the inevitable declaration of war on Sunday 3 September 1939, Wymondham soon had to put some plans into practice.

Evacuees enjoying a Christmas party at the Senior School in December 1940. On the day after war broke out, nearly 1000 evacuee mothers and children had arrived in the town by bus from Great Yarmouth, which they had reached the previous day by boat from Gravesend. During the "Phoney War" many evacuees returned home, but when London was bombed more arrived again, so by September 1941 there were 965 in the town.

Members of the Spooner Row Womens' Institute at a jam-making session in the first week of September 1940. The ladies bought surplus plums, then sold the jam to raise money to purchase Christmas comforts for the troops. In that session the ladies made 3551 pounds of jam with Bessie Maddocks (on the extreme right) making 182 pounds in one day! The Market Cross was a collecting-point for rose hips.

A party of local dignatories watching postmen at work in the sorting office of the new Post Office when it opened on 29 May 1940. Receiving letters from loved ones far away was a morale booster. Harry Clarke, Urban District Council chairman, performed the opening ceremony and stands next to the lady in the left foreground. First on the right, busy sorting, is Martin Wicks.

Pupils at Morley School with their teachers in 1942. Brown paper was stuck across the windows to prevent flying glass causing injuries should a bomb explode in the vicinity. In the hours of darkness, dark material had to cover windows to stop light showing; and as early as November 1939 infringements of the blackout regulations were reported in Wymondham, for which the offenders faced prosecution.

The Wymondham Auxiliary Fire Service in those dark days of June 1940. At the time there was an urgent appeal for recruits, who had to be over age 40. The existing ranks were expected to be considerably depleted by the end of the year as further men were called up for military service. In 1941, the Wymondham Fire Service was transferred to the National Fire Service.

Members of the Royal Observer Corps, followed by the A.R.P. Wardens, parade up Market Street on 28 February 1942, the inaugural day of Warship Week. Leading the way are Arthur Ogden, who is saluting , and Dick Young. The week raised £100,843 and, during the war, the townsfolk collected other vast amounts for the nation's fighting funds through War Charities Weeks, Wings for Victory Weeks, Soldiers' Weeks and other campaigns.

One of the Wymondham First Aid Parties geared up for any emergency. First aid posts and points were situated around the town and a siren to warn of air raids was sited at the police station. Many bombs, including incendiaries, high explosives and one flying bomb, fell in the parish damaging property, but resulting in no loss of life. Pictured are: Back row (left to right) W. Tunaley, Dido Mabbutt (?), W.A. Gosling. Front row: C. Robey, W. Cowles, H. Smith.

Members of the Home Guard Battalion from the Wymondham district who were concerned with transport. Fourth from the left in the back row is Mr Spinks, one of at least two bus drivers in the group. The Local Defence Volunteers were formed in May 1940, but the name was soon changed to the Home Guard. Major Philip Fryer was commanding officer of the Wymondham Platoon, which met at the Drill Hall in Pople Street.

Ground crew members of Hethel's 389th Bomb Group of the United States 8th Army Air Force "sweating it out", as they nervously wait for planes to return from a mission. Americans first came to Hethel in November 1942, the 389th B.G. arriving in June 1943. The group flew 307 missions out of the base over Germany and occupied Europe. Many locals were sad to see the Yanks leave in May 1945.

The American Army Air Force Hospital at Morley taken from the water tower. Built on the site of the Mid-Norfolk Golf Club's course, the hospital was handed to the Americans in September 1943, the 231st Station Hospital moving in the following March. From D Day to the end of 1944, 2,099 patients arrived at the hospital via Wymondham Railway Station and another 1,155 were admitted in 1945.

Local girls with American friends at the Morley hospital. From the left, the girls are Joan Sheldrake, Peggy Oldfield and Joan Bailey, whose parents kept a cycle shop in Bridewell Street. Yanks on cycles were a familiar sight. Many friendships were formed at dances, both in local halls and on the bases, with trucks known as "passion wagons" often transporting the girls to the latter.

At Christmas 1943 American Army Air Force personnel distributed sweets, biscuits and other goodies to over 300 youngsters from the Infant and Junior Schools as they filed past the open front of Alf Harvey's fish shop in Damgate. Youngsters living in the outlying parts of the parish enjoyed a great time at a party on one of the bases.

The Anglo-American Services Club was opened in the former Picture Theatre in Town Green in March 1944 by Colonel Lord Walsingham. The club was run by the Church Army under Captain Brown and, to help make our allies feel at home, it included not only a canteen and recreation room but also American innovations like "shoe-shine parlours". It closed in February 1946.

Chaplain L.W. Wickham from the American Hospital at Morley stands in this group outside the Congregational Church in 1945. On the extreme left is Peter Standley, who was awarded the D.S.C. for helping to sink a heavily armed trawler in a "spirited action" off the Dutch coast two years earlier. Chaplain Wickham sometimes took services at the Church and presented it with an American flag in March 1945. The Free Churches held a service there two months later during the V.E. celebrations. Both V.E. Day and V.J. Day were celebrated with great excitement and relief in the town.

Chapter Six

Postwar Wymondham

I N SOME WAYS WYMONDHAM returned to normality fairly quickly in the immediate postwar years. Taken in the late Forties, the picture shows the annual sports being advertised on a board by the Market Cross and a Service 12 bus awaiting passengers for Norwich. In 1948 at the Secondary Modern School, the Youth Centre was attracting 150 youngsters a week.

However, the new Labour government, which included South Norfolk's Chris Mayhew, faced huge problems and the country suffered some years of austerity. It was 1954 before all rationing completely ended; and the shortage of coal was particularly critical during the terribly severe weather in the first months of 1947. However, the Welfare State and the National Health Service were born and, in a nationwide spate of council house building, over 40 houses and 15 prefabricated bungalows were erected at Silfield.

Built as a memorial to all those who had died in Japanese prisoner of war camps, the present Roman Catholic Church was opened in September 1952.

Mrs Ethel Felstead's tobacconist's and Sunday newsagent's business in Damgate was still flourishing after the war. It had been established by her late husband James around 1925 and operated a lending library with a member's fee of 2d (1p) a week. Walter Cowles helped Mrs Felstead with her Sunday round in the Fifties and took it over on her death in 1955.

Alf Harvey's fish and chip van did excellent business on Wymondham Market Place and in the surrounding villages. Children loved their penny or twopence worth of chips in those once familiar conical bags. Harvey opened his fish and chip shop in Damgate in 1935, the slogan "Alf's is the pla(i)ce" becoming famous throughout the neighbourhood.

In October 1946, the Reverend George Yaxley conducted a service in the smithy in Friarscroft Lane to mark the 150th anniversary of the Baptist Church in Wymondham. In the 19th century the building had served as the Baptist Chapel before becoming Henry Moore's blacksmith's shop. Moore's was one of several smithies in the town in the early 1900s.

The Wymondham Doric Health team which gained third place in a competition at Diss in the Summer of 1947. The Doric Health movement had come to the town in 1937, holding classes in tap dancing and "keeping fit to music" at the Women's Institute Hall on Norwich Road and claiming participation would lead to "good health, beauty, vitality and happiness".

Wymondham Minors take the field at Carrow Road, Norwich in April 1948 for the Norfolk Minor Cup Final, in which they defeated their Sheringham opponents 5-3 after a thrilling period of extra time. Many supporters travelled to the match in a special train. The team was (left to right): C. Lincoln, C. Skipper, G. Nurse, A. Harwood, M. Jermyn. R. Kidd, G. Briggs, E. Darkins, D. Hardy, R. Shiplee and C. Welton. The Minor Cup came to the town again in 1951, 1953 and 1954.

The Wymondham Dell team which won the Norfolk County Bowls Cup (Division 1) in 1946, beating the holders Waterloo Park, Norwich, in the final. The line-up was: Back row (left to right) A. Fielding, B. Bartram, P. Bowden, W . Fulcher, R. George, H. A. Bowles, G. Davey, H. Cann. Front row: R. Howlett, M. A. Norton (hon sec), W. Last (president), A. Brown (captain), W. Cushing. At the time the Dell were said to "have one of the finest greens in the Eastern Counties".

Daisy Shrimpling nailing heads to handles by machine at the Briton Brush Company's factory around 1950. Many workers were bussed to the factory daily from surrounding villages. In 1946 the "Briton", the town's premier employer, had held a celebration evening at the Samson & Hercules House, Norwich, not only to mark the 200th anniversary of its foundation, but also to welcome back 112 employees who had served in the forces.

Pictured in August 1949, Wymondham's famous smock mill at Northfield was a landmark for miles around. Sadly, on 17 February 1950 the mill was destroyed by a terrible fire, which it was believed started in the engine room. Because of the fire-fighting operation, half of the town was on very low water pressure and nearby houses were practically without water at all.

Leo Howes leading for Wymondham Cobras cycle speedway team against Attleborough Aces in 1952. On Summer Sunday afternoons, in the early Fifties, people flocked to the Strayground to cheer on the Cobras, who competed in the Wymondham & District League against such teams as the Aces, Deopham & Hackford Fliers, Hethersett Hornets and Wicklewood & Kimberley Owls.

Children of the Junior School giving a folk dancing display on the Market Place as part of the town's Festival of Britain celebrations in July 1951. Among other events were an Old English Market , the stalls of which can be seen in the picture, displays organised by the Youth Centre cum Evening Institute at the Secondary Modern School and a cricket match between the town's cricket club and a Norwich City F.C. XI.

Wymondham Coronation Committee with their carnival queen and attendants in June 1953. The carnival queen was Janet Crane and her attendants were Christine Walker (left) and Doris Bell. The chairman of the committee was W. A. Ogden (fifth from the right in the back row), while the honorary secretary was Tom Turner (third from the left in the back row). From 1949 Tom Turner held the office of Town Clerk for nearly 40 years and became known as "Mr. Wymondham".

A United Service in the Priory Gardens was one of many events in Coronation week. Among other attractions were sports on the King's Head Meadow, bonfire and firework displays, a fancy dress parade, concerts, dances and teas for the children and old people, who also enjoyed a free film show at the Regal. Like the Festival of Britain, the Coronation celebrations gave the nation a boost after some grim times.

Chapter Seven

The Rocking Fifties

IN NOVEMBER 1959, the Remembrance Day parade, headed by the Band of the 4th Battalion Royal Norfolk Territorial Army, marches to the War Memorial. Five years earlier, Wymondham's British Legion branch had won the Haig Cup for raising the most money in the country for the Poppy Appeal, as well as the Membership Cup for increasing its numbers more than any other branch. Postwar austerity had disappeared and, in the late Fifties, regular trades fairs staged by the Chamber of Trade were indicative of a thriving town. Indeed, in 1955 Wymondham had been described as "one of the happiest market towns" in Norfolk.

Pop music, particularly rock'n'roll, was making headlines and, inspired by the likes of Lonnie Donnegan, skiffle groups, like that formed by drummer Mike Winton at the Abbey Youth Club in 1957, were all the rage.

The local Zetas skiffle group perform their own infectious brand of music at a Baptist Youth Club evening garden party in August 1958. The event was held at the home of Mr and Mrs R. Shorten in Chapel Lane. On the left are Peter Larke (guitar and vocals) and Barry Halford (drums), while on the right are Robert Smith (guitar) and Alan Sidell (bass). The bass was made from a tea chest and broom handle.

Everyone had a swinging time in the Cross Keys when the Keymen were playing. Fans packed the pub for their sessions and reaching the toilet was a major operation! The trio was Charlie Webb, the licensee, (piano), Tony Burton (double bass) and Alan Garwood (accordion). With popular local band the Ace of Clubs often on stage, hundreds were attracted to dances at the Women's Institute Hall.

Handbell ringers at a Harvest Festival service in the Railway Hotel. Harry Sheffield, the licensee and a member of the Urban District Council, instituted the annual event in 1958. The services were often conducted by Rev. J. G. Tansley Thomas, the Vicar, and produce brought along was auctioned for Silfield Church funds. Among the bellringers are Tom Spight (extreme left), William Clover (third from the left) and Harry Tooke (extreme right).

With music provided by the Salvation Army band, the traditional Carol Service around the Market Cross became a major event in the Wymondham calendar during the late 1950s. Walter Cowles's Sunday newsagent's business, Bunn's noted baker's and grocer's shop, Billy Standley's antiques emporium and other retail outlets gave the Market Place a prosperous appearance. In 1965 Cowles's shop was incorporated into the Cross Keys.

A production of "The Farmer's Wife", a lively comedy, presented by the Wymondham Players at the Women's Institute Hall in November 1955. On the right are Doctor Rhoades Buckton and Edna Sturman, who played the farmer and his housekeeper respectively. The players first trod the boards two years earlier and two of their leading lights were Denise Muir (third from the left) and Bob Bagshaw (sitting at the table on the right).

The Wymondham Cricket Club which beat Bracon Ash in the final of the Kimberley Cup in 1958. Wymondham won the cup seven times between 1955 and 1963. The team was back row (left to right):- Keith Bunn, Bob Dack, Ken Percival, Stan Canham, Mike Parsons. Front row: David Postle, Norman Brighton, Steve Cavill, Alan Harwood (capt), Bob Fields and Albert Halstead. After playing many years on the King's Head Meadow, it was their first season at Browick Rec. A brilliant footballer, Percival was Wymondham's finest postwar sportsman.

Dr. Norman Lees, Urban District Council chairman, addresses the annual children's Christmas party, organised by the Rothbury Estate Social Club at the Drill Hall around 1956. Also on the platform is Rev. J. G. Tansley Thomas, Vicar of Wymondham 1953-1973. The social club exemplified the community spirit on the Rothbury Estate and a similar party was held for the old folk. In 1957, the Rothbury Boxing Club was formed and staged a show at the W.I. Hall, which included an exhibition bout featuring local lad Les King and the legendary Ginger Sadd.

The Wymondham Ex-servicemen's Club in 1955. Opened in 1922, it was situated just off the Market Place in Queen's Street. In the mid-1950s, it offered members a fully licensed bar, billiards or snooker and a television room, then a popular facility. Subscriptions were 8s 8d (43p) per annum for ex-servicemen, while honorary members paid 15s (75p). It was demolished in 1963.

Popular John Thompson, the oldest paper boy in Wymondham, working for Ringers, the newsagents, in July 1957. Whatever the weather, he delivered newspapers on a 22 miles round, which included Hethersett, Great Melton and Carleton Forehoe, as well as Wymondham. After delivering papers for 21 years, he took a job at the Co-op brush factory in 1962 when he was then aged 53. A bachelor, John lived in a caravan next to the now demolished London Tavern.

Engineers surveying the scene in October 1957 during the construction of Wymondham's first bypass. Opened in 1958, the bypass only ran between Bait Hill and the Fairland, but was described as the biggest road-building project in Norfolk since the war. It necessitated the demolition of five cottages at the Bait Hill end and the diversion of the Bays and Tiffey Rivers so they joined before crossing the line of the new road.

Chapter Eight

The Swinging Sixties

PETER OLORENSHAW'S 1904 HUMBERETTE leading an amusing parade of decorated vehicles in May 1960. Organised by the Rotary Club, the event was one of many to raise money for World Refugee Year.

There is no doubt that in the Swinging Sixties there was a buzz about Wymondham. Carnivals were held for the first time since 1936, dances were packed at the Women's Institute Hall and the Octopus Youth Club was formed in 1965 at the former Griffin pub. In 1966 the Wymondham Society (later the Wymondham Heritage Society) was founded and in 1967 the Dell Bowling Club opened its first indoor green.

Suddenly everything was happening! A new police station (1963), the Central Hall (1965) and a new fire station on London Road (1967) were all opened, while the town itself experienced unprecedented growth. Hundreds of houses went up in areas like Chapel Lane, Tuttles Lane and Tithe Barn (Orchard Way) and, after modest increases in previous decades, the population jumped by 2609 between 1961 and 1971 to 8513.

Things were swinging at this all-night jazz session, starring Dick Charlesworth's City Gents, in the Women's Institute Hall on Norwich Road during May 1961. In the early Sixties trad boom, Friday evening dances, featuring traditional jazz bands, were being staged regularly at the hall by John Knights, the new licensee of the Cross Keys. However, the "all-nighter" was a one-off, but sparked protests from nearby residents.

In September 1965, the Women's Institute Hall , which had been the venue for most of Wymondham's communal activities since 1927, was put up for sale. It had become redundant with the building of the Central Hall in Back Lane and was demolished to make way for houses. Opened by Lord Mackintosh in December 1965, the Central Hall cost almost £25,000, most of which was raised by the townsfolk.

Mr Philip Fryer opens the Priory Gardens bowling green for old people in July 1960. Mr Fryer was chairman of the presentation fund set up to mark the retirement of Doctor George Gaynor, seen on the right behind the bunting. A much loved G.P. for 38 years and four times chairman of the Urban District Council, Doctor Gaynor had requested that most of the fund be used for the green.

Wymondham Town Reserves at Carrow Road, Norwich, before they lost a keenly contested Norfolk Junior Cup Final 1-0 to Acle in April 1960. Afterwards the teams and officials were entertained to dinner at the Great Eastern Hotel, where the cup and medals were presented. The team was back row (left to right) :- A. Royall (linesman), W. Tunaley (trainer), D. Hagen, R. Riches, M. Parsons, P. Smith, P. Hammond, J. Tillett, F. Hall (secretary). Front row :- M. Barrett, D. Riches, D. Bowell, B. Howes, M. Eke.

Girls of the Guild of St. Agnes processing to the Roman Catholic Church, where they were confirmed by Monsignor Leo Parker, the Bishop of Northampton, in May 1960. Fifty-four candidates, including seven adults, from Wymondham and district as well as Dereham were confirmed by the Bishop, who was making his triennial visitation to the Church. Father M. L. Cowin, the parish priest, assisted at the service and afterwards tea was served in the Church Hall by members of the Catholic Women's League.

A scene from the Passion Play, which was performed in Wymondham Abbey during Lent 1963. The Abbey's magnificent interior proved a superb setting for the scenes from Palm Sunday to the Ascension, which were dramatically portrayed by 70 anonymous local actors. There was a week of evening performances up to and including Good Friday. A less ambition Passion Play had been staged in Wymondham Secondary Modern School's hall six years earlier.

Looking towards the Girl's Secondary Modern School in 1962. A modern mixed "Seniors" school had been established in 1939 off Norwich Road and this became the Boy's Secondary Modern School when the girl's school was opened in November 1958. Now all the buildings are occupied by the mixed Wymondham High School. As the picture shows, horticulture was an important subject in the boy's curriculum.

The Abbey Church fête on the lawns of Abbotsford in Vicar Street during a sunny Saturday afternoon in June 1963. A regular social occasion in the town's calendar, the fête boasted 33 stalls and competitions that year. The drum and bugle band of the junior ratings from H.M.S. Ganges demonstrated marching and countermarching, while the girls and boys of the Secondary Modern Schools gave displays of dancing and physical education respectively.

Looking down Market Street on a wintry Saturday afternoon in January 1963. Barclays Bank's new building, which had opened in July 1962, is on the right, but on the immediate left are two fine Georgian houses which, along with the Ex-servicemen's Club, were sadly demolished later in 1963 to make way for retail units. The nearer of these had housed the Men's Club until its closure in 1959, while next to it was the popular Mary Elizabeth Tearooms which had closed in 1958. The Mary Elizabeth Café had originally started in small Bridewell Street premises during World War Two.

When this picture was taken in 1964, Key Markets had already occupied one of the units built on the developed Market Street site. Others, like Gayton's Fish Bar, soon followed and the development was indicative of much modernisation to shops and businesses in the Sixties.

Staff of Clarke & Co with popular proprietor Harry Clarke, a man prominent in local affairs. The all-purpose store is shown on the right in the picture on page 56 and, like Corstons in Damgate and the Co-op, it was a draper's-cum-grocer's shop. It closed soon after Mr Clarke's death in 1969. On Mr Clarke's left and wearing glasses is Lily Hayes, who joined the drapery department in 1916 and retired from shop work in 1995 shortly before her 93rd birthday!

The historic King's Head Inn on the Market Place looking rather forlorn in January 1963. When Bullards, the brewers, closed the pub in November 1962, the licence had been held by various members of the Goffin family since 1898. The pub had once been Wymondham's social centre and a coaching inn, yet despite many protests it was demolished. Woolworth's store was built on the site in 1980-81.

WYMONDHAM WELCOMES LOTUS

When the world-famous Lotus sports and racing car concern move their headquarters from Cheshunt, Hertfordshire, to a much bigger factory now being built on the former airfield at Hethel, Norfolk, several hundred employees and their families will follow their jobs into East Anglia and be in need of new homes.

Wymondham U.D.C. and Lotus have worked together to stage a special exhibition at the town's Central Hall on Sunday afternoon to introduce the 'newcomers' to the district and give them a hearty welcome. This special supplement has a two-fold aim: to tell Lotus employees something about the area in which they may soon be living, and keep Wymondham and district people well informed of this exciting development on their doorstep.

Renowned for superb personal service in

Town where history and progress live in union

IMAGINE a narrow street of history. On either side the weathered, half-timbered

An extract from a special supplement which appeared in the Norwich Mercury in June 1966 to welcome several hundred employees of Lotus Cars Limited, which was moving to Norfolk from Hertfordshire. Lotus moved to the former Hethel airfield and built a factory, which incorporated some of the hangers and used parts of the old runway as a car test track. The advent of the motor giant was a major boost to the local economy.

In July 1969, the Wymondham town sign, carved by Harry Carter of Swaffham, was unveiled by Ella Bowden, treasurer of the Wymondham Women's Institute for over 30 years. Mrs Bowden stands next to the sign and George Marwood, chairman of Wymondham Urban District Council, is on the left. The sign was presented to the town by the Women's Institute to mark their Golden Jubilee, though the Urban District Council had first considered Mr Carter's plans for a sign in 1957.

Chapter Nine

The Restive Seventies

W. S. HALL & PALMER'S fortnightly auction at their saleground, which was situated between Fairland Street and Bridewell Street, on a Friday in June 1976. Sales, which for a long time had included not only furniture, bric-à-brac and the like but also produce and livestock, had been held there through the century. However, soon after the picture was taken they would move to a new Station Road site.

Nationally the 1970s was a period of considerable unrest, particularly on the industrial front, while locally further new building saw more parts of old Wymondham disappear. Under the unfortunate local government reorganisation of 1974 Wymondham sadly lost its Urban District status and reverted to having a parish council. On the bright side, the town's heart was designated a conservation area "of outstanding architectural and historic interest".

Many more houses were built to accommodate an increasing population and by 1981 70% of houses were owner-occupied. In early 1973 new public toilets were opened beside the car park off Market Street, those in the Market Place having been demolished.

This dilapidated old weaving factory behind 58 Damgate was demolished in 1973, while workers' cottages in the same area, known as Alligator Yard, met a similar fate. Weaving had once been the town's staple trade. The redevelopment trend of the previous decade continued; and on nearby Damgate Hill a row of 16th century houses was pulled down to make way for old people's bungalows.

Rattle Row in March 1977 when the Department of the Environment's inspector decided that South Norfolk District Council could demolish it - despite protests from the Wymondham Society and the Norfolk Society. The terrace, which took its name from the noisy looms, had been built about 1810-1820 to house local weavers. Faced with a chronic housing shortage, the Council built old people's bungalows on the site.

George Harwood's general stores, together with the adjoining buildings in Friarscroft Lane, was pulled down in the early 1970s to make way for flats.

When Kenneth Whitehand closed his Market Street supply stores in 1970 he was described as "the last sizeable independent grocer" in the town, while in 1974 one local commentator remarked, "the growth of supermarkets has caused the death of small businesses and erstwhile shops have been taken over by estate agents". The sympathetic redevelopment of the Chandler's Hill area continued into the 1980s.

The well-stocked Pricerite superstore at its opening in May 1972 on the Norwich Road site of the old Wymondham Laundry, which had closed three years earlier. Covering 35,000 square feet, the store, which later became International then Gateway, was the biggest of its kind in Norfolk and was heralded as the unique "one-stop shopping experience". Fifteen months earlier, shoppers had been grappling with the new decimal currency, which had been introduced.

72

A coach and horses outside the late 15th century Green Dragon Inn in May 1970. Attired in period costume, various personalities, including Anglia T.V.'s Dick Joice, lunched at the pub before taking the coach to Jarrold's store in Norwich. The event was staged to mark the bicentenary of Jarrolds establishing their business in the city. Before the Great War, the Dragon did not serve mild beer and was regarded as "a top peoples' pub".

As a young boy looks on, members of the Wymondham Flower Club prepare for a flower festival at the Abbey Church in September 1972. Two hundred volunteers helped with the festival in different capacities; and over four days there were 10,000 visitors. A record sum of £1,100 was raised for the "cleaning the organ fund". Several successful flower festivals were held in the Abbey during the sixties and seventies.

This lunch for pensioners of the Briton Brush Company at the Abbey Hall in the late 1970s exemplified the camaraderie that existed at the factory. The Abbey Hall was opened in April 1970 to replace the Vicarage Room, which had served the community for over 60 years and had been built of wood and corrugated iron. The Over-60s Club donated £1000 towards the Abbey Hall building fund and made it their home for meetings.

Ted Heath, Conservative leader of the Opposition and former Prime Minister, chats with Eddie Buttolph, long-standing chairman of the Wymondham Chamber of Trade, at a reception in the Abbey Hall in September 1974. John MacGregor, M.P. for South Norfolk, is on the left. The non-political reception was attended by 140 people, representing 70 voluntary organisations, and among them was Brigadier G. C. Gray of Silfield. The brigadier had once been Mr Heath's Commanding Officer in the Territorial Army!

A colourful carnival procession on Monday 6 June 1977 was one of many events to celebrate the Queen's Silver Jubilee. Elsie Capps, chairwoman of the town's jubilee committee, was joined on her ride in the procession by George Mabbutt, who sported a smart uniform. The driver was Horace Wilkinson. Among a tremendous array of floats, one by the Swym committee, portraying "swimming through the ages", won first prize. Swym had been formed a year earlier to raise funds for a pool in the town.

Alf Harvey, a great Wymondham character, was on hand to chat to visitors to the Market Cross, where an exhibition of old photographs was being held over the three days of the Queen's Jubilee celebrations. Attired in his pearly king outfit as a mascot during Norwich City's famous 1958-1959 F.A. Cup run, Alf became almost a national celebrity. Among other jubilee events were a baby show, a children's fancy dress parade and a flower show.

When Sandow's circus, starring Barney the Bear, visited the town in the late 1970s, it featured clowns, jugglers, tumblers, hand-balancing, performers on high stilts and a comedy car. The big top was erected on the Fairland, which for generations had been the traditional site for circuses, fairs and the like. It was way back in 1203 that King John had granted the town the right to hold a fair.

Police Constable John Speakman watching as the Duke of Edinburgh waves from a metallic bronze Lotus Elite as he passes through bunting-bedecked Bridewell Street in October 1979. The Duke had driven from Sandringham and was on his way to the Lotus factory where he was shown round by the legendary Colin Chapman, the chairman. He was most impressed. P.C. Speakman was a reassuring sight on Wymondham's streets - that old-fashioned bobby on the beat.

Chapter Ten

The Volatile Eighties

WHEN THIS 120 foot chimney crashed to the ground in February 1988, it symbolised the sad end of Wymondham's brushmaking. The chimney and the nearby water tower were remnants of the earlier thriving Co-op factory. This business and the Briton Brush Company once employed 1000 townsfolk between them, but all that changed in the 1980s, which began with a boom then ended with a slump. Increasing competition from abroad led to the country importing more goods than hitherto and an influx of cheap brushes from the Far East signalled the demise of the town's brush factories.

On a happier note, the decade saw the opening of the Heritage Museum in an old bakehouse behind the Council Offices in 1984 and victory in a protracted battle against the introduction of car parking fees in 1988. In 1984 the Town Plan consultation document contained "provocative ideas" for developments on the King's Head Meadow, Browick Rec and the Priory Bowling Green. Thankfully, these absurd proposals never came to fruition.

The Co-operative Wholesale Society's brush factory, situated between Chapel Lane and Barnham Broom Road, just prior to its demolition in 1987-1988. Opened in 1922, the factory had also assembled some garden machinery and at its height it had employed 220 people, but at the time of closure in 1983 only 36 employees remained. Later, houses were built on the 13 acre site.

The Lady's Lane brush factory of Briton Chadwick Limited (formerly the Briton Brush Company) shortly before its sale to the Windmill Brush Company in 1982 and subsequent closure three years later. In the foreground are part of an office and the board stores, while next to them is the moulding mill. After closing, the factory was pulled down to make way for housing. Roads called Briton Way and Page's Way are reminders of a flourishing factory that was Wymondham's premier employer.

Clive Clarke (left) and his brother Denis posing outside their Bridewell Street ironmonger's shop on their retirement in November 1981. Their father Frank had set up the firm in 1912 and, after they sold it, the business continued for about 15 years as Frank Clarke (Hardware) Ltd. Also in the picture is Harold Brown, who used to drive the shop's delivery van. The year 1981 also saw Wymondham lose the long established Co-op store.

The Crown pub on the corner of Fairland Street and Friarscroft Lane at the time of its closure in October 1981. Soon afterwards it became the home to fast food outlets. In 1983 the London Tavern on London Road closed and was subsequently demolished, while in the 1990s the Cock and the White Horse were converted to private dwellings. In the picture with the lorry are Ronnie Thurston (right), Charrington's manager, and Horrie Oldfield, the driver.

Preston Avenue's street party in July 1981 to celebrate the Royal Wedding of Prince Charles and Lady Diana Spencer. Fifty children sat down to a tea in the sunshine. Among other parties in a town, festooned with bunting, flags and window displays, were those at Arundel Road and in Alston's barn at Silfield. The Kett's Lodge old folk enjoyed a specially baked cake.

Organised by the Swym Committee, the carnival in June 1981 was one of several such successful events in the 1980s. Coming up Fairland Street in the parade was a Lotus Esprit Turbo car, which appeared that year in the James Bond movie "For Your Eyes Only", while following it was the King family's traction engine. The afternoon's events on the King's Head Meadow included a display by the Medieval Society of Norwich.

The health centre, shown on the right, takes shape on the town's former saleground in March 1982. On the left is the old saleroom, while Elm Terrace is in the background. The centre, which was officially opened by Mrs Patricia Batty-Shaw in February 1983, cost a total of £$\frac{1}{2}$ million and brought all the Wymondham area's health facilities under one roof, including the consulting rooms of the town's six doctors.

John MacGregor, M.P. for South Norfolk (left), and William Armstrong, chairman of Wymondham Town Council, stand either side of a thermometer in May 1982. They were launching a rebuilding fund for the North Wymondham Community Association centre in Lime Tree Avenue, the project being completed by 1985. John Braden, the association chairman, is second from the left. The previous two decades had seen the North Wymondham estate, including shops and a pub, fully established. The Ashleigh First School had been opened at Sheffield Road in 1972.

With captain Mick Weaver holding the ball, Wymondham Rugby Club 1st XV proudly pose in front of their new clubhouse, which was officially opened by English international Dickie Jeeps in April 1983. From its formation in 1972, the club played on a pitch at the High School until moving to its Tuttle's Lane ground in September 1982. Boasting a huge membership and playing at a high level, the club has continued to go from strength to strength.

Wymondham Town F.C. entertaining Great Yarmouth in a Norfolk Senior Cup encounter on the King's Head Meadow in December 1981. Unfortunately the Town went down 3-0, but in the 1981-1982 season they suffered only one defeat in winning promotion from Division 1 of the Anglian Combination. The then recently erected clubroom stands beside the old pavilion, which in 1991 would make way for a further extension incorporating new changing facilities. Meanwhile the Meadow, the Town's home for over 100 years, was levelled in 1987.

Displaying her prize onions is Jill Clarke, who won ten first awards and two trophies at the Wymondham Horticultural Society's annual show at the Central Hall in September 1981. Most of Mrs Clarke's successes came in the vegetable categories. Holding Mrs Clarke's trophies are Fiona Miller, Miss Wymondham, and television cook Patrick Anthony. Two years later Miss Miller flew the flag for the town by winning the Miss Anglia title.

A 22-man manual pump drawn by two greys heads a procession to Wymondham Fire Station in September 1982. The pump had been used by the Wymondham Fire Brigade in 1882 and the parade was one of the events to celebrate the brigade's centenary. Three other ancient pumps, including a six-man manual originally built in 1750, were carried on a lorry. Static displays and demonstrations enthralled the public at the fire station.

Horace Wilkinson in the guise of a monk leads a peasants' procession to the Market Cross on Kett Day in July 1985. In the middle of the leading trio is Brenda Ford, the Town Mayor, while on her right is Philip Richardson. A remarkable day of events and street entertainments, organised by Robert Kett Middle School headmaster Stan Kelly and the Rotary Club, saw Wymondham turn the clock back to Tudor times to celebrate the rebellion in 1549 led by its most famous son. Townsfolk sported period dress and some 200 Ketts turned up for the occasion.

The Wymondham Sapphires were the twirling majorettes who captivated spectators at carnivals, fetes and the like in the 1980s. Here they are performing during Kett Day. Formed in 1980 as the North Wymondham Majorettes, they practised at the High School and in 1982 won a major trophy at Sudbury. From then on, they competed with success in regional and national competitions with Vicky Reynolds and Helen Brown shining at an international level in solo events.

Actor Bill Pertwee of Dad's Army fame addresses a 700 strong crowd on Wymondham Railway Station plain in October 1989. Mr Pertwee unveiled a plaque commemorating the restoration of the station by local businessman David Turner, who is standing behind him. Two years earlier Mr Turner had found the unmanned station in a derelict state, but with loving restoration he turned it into an award-winning tourist attraction with a Brief Encounter tearoom.

The Wymondham Market Cross during its major restoration in 1988-1989, which cost £94000. A public appeal, headed by Philip Richardson the Town Mayor, raised £17,710, the balance coming from grants. Extensive repairs to the upper storey included plastering and treatment of the woodwork, but there was controversy over the lime-washing of the timber frames. However, this was later rectified and the restored cross was officially reopened by journalist John Timpson in October 1989. In 1990 the Cross became the town's tourist information centre.

Chapter Eleven

The Bustling Nineties

A HURRICANE OF ACTIVITY swept through Wymondham in the 1990s; and the town centre traffic management scheme was a prime example. Taken in September 1995, the picture shows work on the scheme, which cost £640,000. A one-way system, traffic calming measures and a new look Market Place, laid with granite setts and with parking prohibited, were all features.

Many people moved to pleasant Norfolk during the decade and extra housing was needed to accommodate them. Wymondham's contribution was mainly the Hart's Farm development. With people living longer, the final phase of the town's housing scheme for the elderly at Ogden Close was completed in 1995 and another medical centre was opened in 1998. The new bypass came into use in 1996.

Nationally new housing and road-building has sadly resulted in large areas of countryside disappearing with wildlife under threat. At least in Wymondham efforts have been made to minimise the impact with a new habitat for great crested newts, countryside walks and a nature reserve at Toll's Meadow.

Looking east from Park Lane to Silfield Road during construction of the £16.5 million Wymondham to Besthorpe A11 bypass in early 1995. Work started on the 5.4 mile dual carriageway in February 1994, but it was hampered by protesters and the extremely wet Summer that year. It was finally completed and opened by the roads minister John Watts on 22 March 1996. The bypass took through traffic away from Wymondham, but brown "Historic market town" signs had to be erected to encourage tourists into it.

Wharton's Court off Market Street in the course of its redevelopment in 1996. Inspirational architect Peter Codling turned a cluster of dilapidated buildings into an attractive little precinct of specialist shop units. Codling's planning expertise played a large part in the Bridewell restoration referred to on page 91. Helped by the "Brighter Wymondham" campaign, the year 1996 saw Norfolk's Best Kept Town Award captured for the first time for 20 years .

Cycling champion Chris Boardman officially opened the fine Wymondham Leisure Centre on Norwich Road in October 1992. In the picture Boardman stands between Charles Leather (left) of South Norfolk District Council and Steve Goddard, the centre's first manager. In front is Richard Leather and the LotusSport superbike, built at Hethel, on which Boardman had won a gold medal at the Olympic Games in Spain. The £1.5 million centre, funded entirely by South Norfolk Council, soon became the hub of many sporting and leisure pursuits.

The last picture show at the Regal in June 1993 saw proprietor Les King deep in thought. Having been the manager since 1966, perhaps he was reflecting that if the crowds who packed the cinema that night had supported it regularly in the past, closure would not have been necessary. But dwindling attendances, sound problems and the Norwich multiplex threat apparently all had their effect. The final movie shown was "Bodyguard", starring Kevin Costner and Whitney Houston.

Wymondham Dell's international bowls player John Ottaway with an amazing haul of desirable silverware in 1990. In that year Ottaway captured the British Isles Bowls Association outdoor singles cup, standing at the front, to add to the others, including the tall English Bowling Association outdoor singles cup, which he had won in 1989. He took that All-England title again in 1996. In 1990 he officially opened the Bert Warren pavilion dedicated to a former president of the tiptop Dell club.

Wymondham runners set out on a training run before the 1996 London Marathon. Wymondham Athletic Club was formed as a jogging club in 1978, but members now compete in cross-country, track and field events, as well as road races. The club has over 100 members, nearly half of them women, and organises five Wymondham - based road races every year. Eva Osborne (4th from the left in the front row) has won medals in veteran athletics events at county, national and international level.

A magical Dickensian Evening on a December Thursday in 1994. The photograph taken from the steps of the Market Cross shows a funfair in full swing and various stalls on the Market Place. For many years a carol service had been held around the Market Cross, but it was not until 1986 that the first Dickensian Evening was organised by the Wymondham Lions. Staged throughout the 1990s, the evening's events invariably included the switching on of the Christmas lights, the arrival of Santa Claus and carol singing.

The queue for the filming of B.B.C. T.V's popular "Antiques Roadshow" programme on a Thursday in March 1995. About 5,000 people turned up to have their pieces valued by the experts in the main sports hall at Wymondham Leisure Centre. The doors did not open until 10.00 a.m, though the first "customer" had arrived from Sheringham three hours earlier. The "Antiques Roadshow", together with a "Songs of Praise" programme from the Abbey Church, publicised the town nationwide.

The Duke of Gloucester chats with Horace Wilkinson, Wymondham Heritage Society chairman, before unveiling a plaque to officially open the restored Bridewell at Norwich Road in May 1996. Accompanying the Duke is Sir Timothy Colman, Lord Lieutenant of Norfolk, while Jenny Chamberlain, the Town Mayor, looks on. Mr Wilkinson was a key figure in the £400,000 project which saw the Bridewell converted to house the Citizens' Advice Bureau, the Red Cross, special housing and the award-winning Wymondham Heritage Museum.

Prince Charles, accompanied by Canon Brian Gant, the Vicar, leaves Wymondham Abbey after attending a Music in Country Churches Trust concert on a Sunday in May 1997. There had also been a concert on the Saturday, but the Sunday event featured the English Chamber Orchestra with director and violinist Pinchas Zukerman. The Prince himself had originally suggested a music weekend at the Abbey, which he had visited informally in 1992.

Diana Hockaday, Chairman of Norfolk County Council, surrounded by children from Browick Road County First School in June 1997. Gareth Worf, on Mrs Hockaday's right, had just won a competition to produce a design to go on special plates underneath new 20 m.p.h. speed limit signs on Browick Road and Gunton Road. In 1997, hard-working Mrs Hockaday, county member for Wymondham, became the first person from the town to take the chair of the Norfolk County Council since its inception in 1889.

Coming down from the old Wymondham to Forncett railway line on the opening day of the Lizard circular walk in April 1997. This walk and others like the Tiffey Valley one, which was opened in November 1995, were established as a result of co-operation and goodwill between the land-owners, the local authorities and other bodies. On the right at the front are David Crowe, former Town Clerk, and Jenny Chamberlain, the Mayor, whose untimely death in 1999 was a big blow to the town.

A scuba-diving display during the official opening before invited guests of Wymondham's £2.3 million swimming pool in April 1999. The 93,000-gallon pool with its 180-seater spectator gallery was a dream come true for members of the Swym committee, like veteran campaigner Denise Muir, who had been raising funds since 1976. Swym donated £90,000, matched by the Town Council, while huge contributions came from the District Council and the Lottery Sports Fund.

A diesel multiple unit makes the first passenger run from Wymondham to Dereham for 30 years on 2 May 1999. Several years of dedicated work by members of the Mid-Norfolk Railway Preservation Trust, together with generous support from Breckland and South Norfolk Councils, made it possible. Freight trains were given the go-ahead some months before the Rail Inspectorate approved public services. Wymondham Abbey Halt was built near the Cavick crossing, but eventually it is hoped to link with the main line station.

A FEW INTERESTING FACTS AND FIGURES

Selected key dates in the Millennium prior to 1900

c1000   Sizeable Saxon settlement with a church near the site of the present Abbey Church. By 1066 the town comprised 15 manors, held till then by Stigand, the last Saxon Bishop of East Anglia.

1107   Foundation of the Priory by William d'Albini, who became Earl of Arundel.

1174   Chapel of St. Thomas à Becket (now Library) founded.

1203   Weekly Friday market and Winter fair established by Charter of King John.

1389   Thomas Walsingham, later Prior, recorded that various miracles were wrought by a cross on the public highway at Wymondham.

1440   Charter of Henry VI confirmed the right to a Friday market and two fairs.

1445   Parishioners granted right to build West Tower of Abbey Church following a lengthy dispute with monks.

1448   Monastery elevated from a priory to the status of an abbey.

1538   Dissolution of the Abbey.

1549   Kett's Rebellion against injustices, including the inclosure of common land, ends in defeat. Robert Kett hung from Norwich Castle and brother William from the West Tower of Wymondham Church.

1559   Grammar School founded (closed 1903).

1598   A bridewell exists (keeper paid £2 per annum).

1615   Great Fire destroys 327 homes worth £14,000 and public buildings valued at £1,000.

1617-18 Present Market Cross built on site of one destroyed in the Great Fire.

1631   Severe outbreak of plague. Norwich citizens contribute £103.5.7 (£103.28) for relief of Wymondham.

1785-87 New Bridewell built on lines laid down by John Howard, prison reformer.

1801   Bad fever and smallpox outbreak.

1836   Six hundred weaving looms recorded in town.

1845   Railway arrives with the station built on the Brandon to Norwich line.

1882   Volunteer Fire Brigade formed and Market Street fire station built a year later.

1886   S. D. Page & Sons, the Norwich brushmakers, move to Wymondham.

1894   Parish Council (and Forehoe Rural District Council) established.

Population of Wymondham

Throughout the millennium Wymondham has been an important place in the county; and at the time of the Domesday survey (1086) the population can be estimated at 1,620. By about 1600 the figure was well over 2,000 and in 1747 Robert Cremer, the Vicar, recorded that there were 3,213 people in the parish. The census of 1881 put the number at 4566. In the 20th century the population has been as follows:-

1901 - 4,731	1931 - 5,017	1961 - 5,904	1991 - 10,869
1911 - 4,794	1941 - no census	1971 - 8,513	1999 - 11,700
1921 - 4,814	1951 - 5,665	1981 - 9,759	(estimate).

County Councillors for Wymondham in the 20th Century

1900 - Earl of Kimberley (Ind)
1901 - E. W. R. Clarke (Ind)
* 1907 - W. B. Fryer (Ind)
1922 - Earl of Kimberley (Lab)
1925 - Major Leslie Fletcher (Con)
* 1931 - Mrs Ethel Gooch (Lab)
1946 - Earl of Kimberley (Ind)
1949 - Dr. George C. Gaynor (Con)
1952 - Jack. R. Boddy (Lab)
* 1955 - Dr. Harold G. Hudson (Ind)
1964 - Herbert E. Wilson (Lab)
1970 - John W. Meadows (Con)
1973 - Anthony R. W. Knights (Lab)
1977 - Robert. C. H. Bunn (Con)
1981 - John Jackson (Lab)
1983 - Mrs Brenda. L. Ford (Con)
1985 - Anthony. K. Tibbitt (Lib/SDP)
1989 - Mrs Diana Hockaday (Lib)
* Became aldermen after their term

Members of Parliament representing Wymondham in the 20th Century

Mid Norfolk Constituency

1895 - Frederick Wilson (Lib)
1906 - Lord Wodehouse (Lib)
1910 - William Boyle (Con)

South Norfolk Constituency.

1918 - Hon W.H. Cozens - Hardy (Con - Lib coalition)
1920 - George Edwards (Lab)
1922 - Major T. W. Hay (Con)
1923 - George Edwards (Lab)
1924 - James Christie (Con)
1945 - Christopher Mayhew (Lab)
1950 - Peter Baker (Con)
1955 - John Hill (Con)
1974 - John MacGregor (Con)

Con = Conservative. Lab = Labour. Lib = Liberal.

Wymondham Town Council

William Fryer became chairman of the parish council in 1898 and held the office until a few months before his death in April 1926. In 1935, Edwin Gooch became the first chairman of the newly created Urban District Council and held the office for most of the period until the end of the war. Ethel, his wife, became the council's first lady member (1935) and its first lady chairman (1951). Doctor George Gaynor was appointed chairman on four occasions, the first being in 1946. In 1984, William Armstrong became Wymondham's first mayor of what again since 1974 has been a parish council. Philip Richardson was twice chairman and twice mayor, while Stephen Buckton was four times mayor.

Vicars of Wymondham Parish Church in the 20th Century.

1898	The Hon Archibald Parker.	1973	Canon George Hall.
1905	Daniel Collyer.	1988	Canon Grant Welch.
1911	Samuel Martin - Jones.	1989	John Barnes.
1932	Canon Frederic Jarvis.	1995	Canon Brian Gant.
1953	Canon James G. Tansley Thomas.		

Other East Anglian titles available from
Nostalgia Publications

TITANIC - THE NORFOLK SURVIVORS
John Balls
The stories of the five Norfolk survivors of this historic disaster

THE HOBBIES STORY
Terry Davy
Over 100 years of the history of the well known fretwork company

MEMORIES OF NORFOLK CRICKET
Philip Yaxley
200 years of history of Norfolk Cricket

LARN YARSELF NORFOLK
Keith Skipper
A comprehensive guide to the Norfolk dialect

LARN YARSELF SILLY SUFFOLK
David Woodward
A comprehensive guide to the Suffolk dialect

LARN YERSALF NORTHAMPTONSHIRE
Mia Butler and Colin Eaton
A comprehensive guide to the Northamptonshire dialect

MIGHTA BIN WUSS
Tony Clarke
The hilarious adventures of the Boy Jimma

TATTERLEGS FOR TEA
David Woodward
More Suffolk Dialect in Yarns and Verse

KID'S PRANKS AND CAPERS
Frank Reed
Nostalgic recollections of childhood

RUSTIC REVELS
Keith Skipper
Humorous country tales and cartoons